<u>Business Lessons For</u>

<u>Success</u>

What they will never teach you in school, and you need to know, to be successful in the Business World

By Antonio Paez

Book Title: Business Lessons For Success

To My Dear Wife, Ana T., Who has Carried Me through The Valleys, and To My Children Carolina, Carlos, Ana Maria, and Luisa who inspire me, and my precious Granddaughter Sophia for the joy she radiates.

"Wisdom is not a product of schooling, but the lifelong attempt to acquire it."

Albert Einstein

Introduction

This book aims to partially fill a void in our education when it comes to common business know-how. Students may go through high school and college, learning detailed information on a particular subject of interest, but seldom do they touch on the key business principles and concepts that will govern how their knowledge will be used over the following years.

While it is impossible to provide a masters degree in business and finance in a few pages, I will do my best to bring to you in the next pages, in simple terminology, certain tips and primers on business, that will give you a basis for further exploration and learning.

I have tried to focus on some of the issues that become second nature as you move through the business world, but are often not taught in formal learning environments.

I hope, through this book to bring you useful business knowledge that will help, balance, and protect you, as you move forward.

Have faith, and good luck...

"You have to learn the rules of the game; and then you have to play better than anyone else."

Albert Einstein

Chapter 1

The Secret to Business Success

There is one key secret to being successful in business and that is… There is no secret to success. It all depends on you! Each of you is more than well equipped to run a business. You already have all the tools you need to succeed.

There are, however, four factors that are keys to being successful. They are known as the four M's, standing for:

- **Mindset**
- **Money**
- **Marketing**
- **Management.**

Let's spend some time on each…

Mindset

You must have confidence, persistence, and passion, in your endeavor. Train your mind to never give up, and push forward with energy.

As in the case of an athlete, who, on the verge of losing the match, comes back and wins. You must be passionate about victory, have the persistence to stay in the struggle, and have the confidence that you can be successful. Your mind can overcome every situation; you just have to have the mindset to do so.

Success does not mean not failing; it means, learning from failure. Most successful businessmen or women have had their ample share of failures. It is part of the learning process, and makes you wiser. For example, in the last few years, I invested a lot of money in real estate, having done the necessary due diligence, and assuming that it was the safest form of investment. As we well know, the real estate market collapsed and the investments were lost. Does this make me afraid to invest in this type of business? No, but, I certainly have learned many hard lessons from this.

I accept the failure and the mistakes, and move on with new wisdom and energy.

Money

In business, cash is king. He who has the cash has the staying power. The greatest cause for business failures is that they run out of cash. By cash, I mean funds available to carry the business through a difficult time. I would recommend having a minimum of one year cash reserves available.

In the case of the current recession, the crisis has surpassed three years, and the reserves on hand, for my company, were one and a half years. I attempted to maintain normal operations till the cash ran out. The lesson to be learned here is that, in addition to having the cash reserves, reduce operations to the bare minimum immediately when the difficulty period begins. No one knows how long these downward cycles can last, so adapt your business immediately, to stretch the survival capability.

Another tactic frequently used in business, is collecting on your sales, before paying the vendors. For example, a supermarket sells its' goods to the public for immediate cash, but usually agrees to pay its vendors within 30 days. In this way, it always has cash available, and in some cases earns more money from the use of this cash during the holding period than in selling the product.

Be very cautious in spending money even when times may be good. Be just as cautious in spending a penny in good times, as you would be in bad times. It is easy to get sloppy with expenditures during good times.

Many small businesses spend enormous amounts of money on consultants, marketing firms, and public relations firms. These services are over-rated, and provide information that can be obtained directly by you as a business owner more efficiently and at lower costs. In most cases, you can sell yourself better than others can sell you, and you can analyze your problems, with depth of knowledge of your business, better than outsiders. Use your intuition with confidence.

Marketing

All businesses must know how to market their product. If they are good marketers of their product they will prosper, if not, they will wither away.

Always ask yourself who your target customer is, then find the best way to reach him, and convince him of your products' benefit and value.

Marketing training and education are a must in today's world. There are many techniques and tactics for marketing successfully... take the time to study and learn these. Good marketing is very product specific. A successful strategy to market one product may be the totally wrong marketing technique for another product, depending on the channel necessary to reach the target customer.

I prefer to sell a service or product on the basis of quality and value, not price. A supermarket sells a few items based on price to lure the customer in and sell him higher profit margin items.

Selling a product on the basis of quality and value often leads the customer to question the price. You must be prepared to justify your position and use it to stand firm on your terms. I often am faced by a customer who states: "I have proposals from others at lower prices."

My response almost always is: "I'm sorry that I misunderstood, I thought you were looking for the best quality and value, not the lowest price. I can give you a few more names of companies that will give you an even better price than you have. My clients choose me because of the quality and the value I deliver." Seven times out of ten, they accept my terms and conditions. Be prepared, and deliver on your value and quality. If you deliver on your promise, you will probably have a customer for life, and remember, it is a lot less expensive to conserve an existing customer, than to get a new one. Take constant care of your existing customers.

Whenever possible make as many sales yourself as you can. Few people will sell the product with as much passion and conviction as you have.

It is fundamental to know and understand your customer well. Most successful companies make all new employees begin their careers interacting directly with the customer.

Management

By management, I mean, have the right resources to provide you with timely and useful data. With the enormous amounts of available in today's world, you must filter and select relevant information for decision making to improve your business.

Spend the time to determine what information is useful and important in your business, and then use people and/or systems to provide in that form.

Remember the term GIGO (garbage in, garbage out), if the information you use to make the decision is based on poor or bad research, the results of your decision based on this information will also be poor. Always question the quality the source, validity, and methodology used to interpret data. A good decision based on defective information is really a bad decision.

I recall an anecdote of Henry Kissinger, ex Secretary of State, requested of a student, an important research paper. The paper was returned three times to the student, each time with bold red annotations, that said: Deficient, Rewrite! Finally the student approached his professor, and said. "I have rewritten the paper three times, I cannot improve on it any further", to which Kissinger replied: "Good, then now I will read it." Cruel, but effective...

In summary, be quick and wise to react to external situations, and always spend the money as if you were going through difficult times. Failure is a part of growth; Learn from it, and push ahead with renewed strength. Take the time to determine who your target customer is and apply good marketing strategies to reach him effectively.

Surround yourself with good systems and people to provide relevant information for wise decisions.

Above all, know that you have it within you to be a successful professional and /or business owner.

"Think; It is what to do when you don't know what to do."

Albert Einstein

Chapter 2

Habits and Tips on Business Professionalism

As our experience in business grows over time, we learn certain do's and don'ts. Here are some lessons from experience, that if incorporated early on will save time in that learning track.

Note Taking

Memories, in the business dealings arena, are short; always take notes. Make notes of everything that may be useful or pending at some future date. As you meet with clients, employees, suppliers, and bosses, many things will be discussed and stated. Usually, nobody will object to your note taking. In today's smart electronic world, those notes can be easily transcribed and carried on any mobile device for quick access.

Power is in information, and your effectiveness will be enhanced greatly if you have the information trail at your fingertips. It is very helpful to pull out last meeting's notes and be able to say: "… last time we met on…we concluded that you would do… what progress have you made?" Generally, the person who has the best records, will have the upper hand in the next meeting or phone conversation.

Treat Everyone with Respect

Each job that each person does is important. You must respect each person and the work they do. Someday, you will be in a higher position in the totem pole in a company; this is not a license to treat people under you poorly. You may still have anger or disappointment with a co worker, but, remember to keep your focus on the issue, and not on the individual. Do not degrade or reduce the value of the contribution made by any individual to the organization.

Repeat Successful Processes

As you grow in business experience, you will find that certain steps will lead to successful outcomes. These vary from individual to individual, however if you can study and isolate the particular steps that worked well for you, they will probably work again if repeated. Over time, you will find certain individual patterns work well for you, and that they can be applied across different industries. Spend the time to analyze and find the patterns that work with you, and the probabilities of future successes increases.

Be Prepared

This Boy Scout motto has proved invaluable over time. The better prepared an individual is for any situation, the better the outcome will be. The best way to learn to be prepared is to constantly be asking yourself: "What if…?" By asking yourself this question, you will look for solutions, and be better equipped to handle it. Better prepared individuals can react better, faster and smarter when the need arises.

Be Organized

Organization will save you a lot of time. There are many tools in the marketplace to keep you organized, but ultimately it will depend on dedicating the time to put things in order from the beginning, to save a lot of time later. Folders are probably the easiest way to keep papers and subjects organized. They are cheap and easily managed.

Today's smart phones and software programs, such as Microsoft's One Note, are great for organizing schedules and information. It takes time to find a system to organize that will work well for your particular needs, but the sooner you find it, the more time and energy you will save over the long run.

Be Prompt

Always be on time. Common business protocol requires that you learn to be on time. Being on time anywhere requires planning, organizing and being prepared, so in a certain sense it is a part of some of the previous things we have covered. Train yourself to make it a habit. Others will respect you for it, and you respect others by doing it.

Be Patient

It is important to understand that people move at different speeds. This does not mean that they will not achieve a goal, it just means that it might take them longer to get there. Be patient and take the time to explain things well to others. Not everyone moves at your speed, and you must give them room to move at their own speed. Patience can make the difference between a misunderstood task, and a successful one.

Delegate

Delegation is the ability to assign certain tasks to other people in order to use your time in a more efficient way. You must learn when it is appropriate to delegate, how to delegate, and how to follow up on delegation. If any of the above is not done properly, problems will arise. Find those certain tasks that you do, that can be done by others in the same or even in a better way. Those are the tasks you should delegate. When you delegate a task it is fundamental that you make the other person understand very clearly what you want him to do, and how you want it done. The more time you spend in explaining and assuring understanding, the more probable it will be done as you ask. Finally, you must periodically follow up that the task is being done well and within the guidelines you established.

Good delegation is a necessity in business; poor delegation will lead to many problems in the future.

Focus on the Details

There is a fine line in business between focusing on the details and micro-managing. Micro-managing is getting involved with every minor detail of someone else's task. Focusing on the details, means determining the key factors in a process and making sure these are executed successfully. You want to focus on the details, not micro-manage. By learning to do this effectively, you will greatly improve on the chances of a task being completed successfully, without having to control every step of the process.

To Do List

As part of becoming better organized, you will find time to be your most precious asset. As your responsibilities grow, you will find a need to be efficient and organized with your time. A *To Do List*, is a simple tool that allows you to plan the tasks you want to do, organize the time in which you will do them, and keep track of the completed ones. Try to end each day with a *To Do List* for the next day. This will help also in maintaining your focus on the pending issues, and in being better prepared for the next day.

Integrity and Ethics

At some point in time you will find yourself tempted to bend the rules, usually for some form of monetary gain. Don't do it! Always be straight and ethical in your dealings. In many cases, siding with integrity will lead you to lose money or other valuable assets, but over the long run you will find yourself a better person because of it. You will have more respect for yourself and have the knowledge that you have acted correctly. In today's world, greed seems to be all around us, and the message seems to be greed is good. But, do not be fooled, there is no price to be paid for holding your head up and being able to say: "I acted correctly". We all know the difference between good and bad, and you will be faced with crises in your life where there will be the easier "bad" road available. At these indecision points, be decisive in going down the "good" road, no matter what the price is. It will usually bring some pain to choose this route, but you will earn the title of honorable businessman. This is the best title you can carry with you throughout your business life.

Chapter 3

Financial Statements Primer

Every executive and business owner must know how to read useful information from financial statements. This chapter is a short summary of the basics. As in the case of Marketing I consider that a finance/accounting course is a must as a part of your education.

The three most important financial statements are:

- **the balance sheet**
- **the profit and loss statement (P&L)**
- **the cash flow statement**

Most other financial statements are, in some form or another, support or supplemental material for one of the three basic statement types. Important information can be derived from each of these reports. With practice you will learn how to interpret these statements thoroughly and what items should set off an alarm.

Balance Sheet

A balance sheet is a photograph of the financial standing of a business at a certain moment in time. Usually a balance sheet will have a date such as the end of a month or end of a year.

The balance sheet is used to indicate the financial health of a company and its' ability to meet its' upcoming obligations, such as loans, interests, and taxes.

This statement is divided into two side by side columns. The left column lists what the business owns (referred to as assets), the right column lists what the business owes (referred to as liabilities) and the capital contribution by shareholders. The total of the right column and the left column are equal. In the case where total liabilities are less than total assets, then owner capital will be positive.

Below, I include a sample balance sheet that will help you understand the items that are included in each side.

Sample Balance Sheet for Company A

Statement date: December 31, xxxx

Assets		Liabilities	
Current Assets (duration < 1 yr)		Current Liabilities (pay < 1 yr)	

Cash in banks	$1,000	Loan on auto (due < 1 yr)	$700
Accounts receivables	$150	Loan to bank	$100
Laptop computer	$300	Taxes due	$50
Auto (1 year value)	$1,000	Money owed to vendors	$100
Goodwill (value of name < 1 yr)	$200	Electric bill due	$50
Office supplies	$50		
Product Inventory	$200		
Total C.A.	**$3,000**	**Total C. L.**	**$1,000**
Long Assets (duration> 1 yr)		Long term Liabilities (due > 1 yr)	
Saving Certificate > 1 yr	$300	Loan owed on building	$4,500
Auto (remainder of life value)	$1,000	Loan on car (pay > 1 yr)	$1,000
Building (less depreciated value)	$5,000	Loan on office furniture	$500
Office	$700		

furniture (value remaining)			
Total L.T. Assets	**$7,000**	**Total L.T. Liabilities**	**$6,000**
		Total Liabilities	**$7,000**
		Shareholder Capital	
		Shareholder Investment	$3,000
Total Assets	**$10,000**	**Total Liabilities and Capital**	**$10,000**

Some of the information that can be obtained from this balance sheet:

- The company has enough money to cover its' current obligations (current assets exceed current liabilities).

- In case of emergency, the company has enough cash on hand to cover all its loans due in this next year(sometimes referred to as acid test).

- Money owed to suppliers, taxes, and utilities, is reasonable and indicates that there are no large old bills owed to them.

- The company has more assets that the obligations on loans.

Profit & Loss

The P&L statement is a reflection of the activity of the company over a period of time. Its' duration is usually on one month or one year. Sometimes it is shown as a column for each month and a total column to reflect the year. This statement is used to determined if the business is generating a monetary profit or loss on its' sales, once the expenses are deducted.

Below, I include a sample P & L that will help you understand the items that are included.

Sample P & L for Company A

Statement date: For the month ending on October 31, xxxx

Sales	
Sales of Product A	$5,000
Sales of Product B	$3,000
Total Sales	$8,000
Cost of Goods Sold (also known as COGS, direct cost of items sold)	$3,000
Gross Profit (Profit from sales that can be applied to general expenses of business	$5,000
Expenses	
Salaries to employees and owner	$2,000
Utilities and Insurance	$500
Taxes and Loan interest	$100
Rent	$300
Office supplies	$50
Miscellaneous expenses	$50
Total Expenses	$3,000
Net Profit	$2,000

Some of the information that can be obtained from this P&L:

- The company is generating a profit of 25% on sales.

- Salaries are a reasonable 20% of sales.

- The business is generating a salary to the owner for his work at the business, plus additional profit as the owner.

- The company is generating enough money from sales to cover all its' obligations, including taxes.

P& L's can be cash basis or accrual basis. Most P&L's are on an accrual basis, indicating that expenses are reflected as they occur, and not necessarily as they are paid (cash basis). In the example above the utilities for the month are reflected, although it is possible that, for example, the electric and the water bills for the month have not been paid yet.

The Cash Flow Statement

The cash flow statement measures the actual cash on hand and cash generated from the business on a monthly or yearly basis. As with the P&L, sometimes it is shown as a column for each month and a total column to reflect the year.

Below I include a sample cash flow statement for three months that will help you understand the items that are included.

Sample Cash Flow for Company A

Statement date: For the three months ending on October 31, xxxx

	Aug.	Sept.	Oct.
Cash BOM (Beginning of Month)	$1,000	$500	$2,500
Cash received from sales	$2,000	$2,500	$1,500
Total	$3,000	$3,000	$4,000
Electric (paid)	$500	$0	$500
Water (paid)	$200	$0	$200
Rent (paid)	$500	$500	$500
Insurance and taxes(paid)	$500	$200	$300
Vendors (paid)	$300	$300	$200
Interest (paid)	$500	$0	$500
Total Cash Out	$2,500	$1,000	$2,500
Net Cash Flow for Month	-$500	$2,000	-$1,000
Cash EOM (End of Month)	$500	$2,500	$1,500

Some of the information that can be obtained from this cash flow statement:

- The company is generating a positive cash flow.

- Some months money paid out exceeds money received so a reserve is required for these months.

- Note that the cash flow at the end of the month is the same as the beginning of the following month.

- The company receives a fairly steady cash flow from its' sales.

Conclusion

The three financial statements provide a good financial indication of the health of the business. As your experience with financial statements grows so will your ability to read more information from each.

Many companies that require providing their financial statements to external entities or shareholders have their statements audited. Audited financial statements have been validated by specialized accounting firms to ensure items are reflected to certain standards, and the numbers have been checked to reduce the possibility of fraudulent reporting. It is a way for a shareholder to have greater assurance of the accuracy of the financial standing of the company he has invested in.

Financial statements projected into the future are referred to as Pro-forma statements. It is not unusual when requesting a business loan from a bank that they will require in addition to historical financial statements, a Pro Forma P&L and a Pro Forma Cash Flow.

Spend the time to study accounting and finance; it is necessary in today's business world, and will help you keep track of the health of the company.

"Any fool can make things bigger, more complex, and more violent. It takes a touch of genius - and a lot of courage – to move in the opposite direction."

Albert Einstein

Chapter 4

Decision Matrix

The decision matrix is a tool to facilitate decision making. Decision making is often a subjective process and this methodology provides a way organize and quantify this subjective process.

Key Points:

- Tool to facilitate decision making
- Allows one to quantify decisions that are usually difficult resolve
- Organize and quantify a subjective process

Process:
Setup a matrix or table in the following way:

	Column1	Column2	Column3	Column4	Column5	Column6	Column7
	Relevant	Importance	Option A	Option A	Option B	Option B	
	Factor	of this issue	1 to 5	weighted	1 to 5	weighted	
		1 to 5	5 best	=col 2 x col3	5 best	=col 2 x col3	
		5 most					
		important					
				Total A		Total B	
				weighted		weighted	

The larger total represents best choice.
This is very useful for group or family decisions
Each individual can list their factor of influence
and a consensus is done on weight and benefit.

Example:

Which college to choose:							
Relevant Factors	Importance	School A	Weighted School A	School B	Weighted School B	School C	Weighted School C
Education Quality	5	5	25	4	20	3	15
Cost	4	3	12	3	12	4	16
Closeness to home	2	1	2	2	4	5	10
Need a car	2	4	8	3	6	5	10
Climate	1	5	5	3	3	3	3
Cost of life	4	2	8	1	4	2	8
Dorm life	3	4	12	2	6	3	9
Scholarship	5	5	25	5	25	2	10
Size of Campus	1	1	1	4	4	4	4
Travel cost	2	3	6	3	6	5	10
Entertainment	1	1	1	2	2	2	2
Total			105		92		97
Best option: School A							

The more time that is spent on determining all the affecting factors and their importance, the more accurate the result.

Chapter 5

Arbitrage

The concept of arbitrage is a simple one, however, it is used in some of the most complicated transactions on Earth.

Arbitrage, simply put, is buying an asset at one price, adding some value to it, and reselling it; hopefully at a profit. The value added can be a service, such as time or knowledge, or adding some material to modify and improve the product.

An example of an arbitrage operation where a service is added would be the case of Amy, an expert on cooking knives, going from flea market to flea market looking for knives. When she finds a Michel Bras boning knife for $350, she buys it, and then re sells it to a chef for $600. By adding her knowledge and time to find the knife, she has generated an attractive arbitrage profit.

An example of a material added arbitrage would be, the case of John buying an 18k gold and amethyst solitaire ring from an estate sale. John changes the stone to an emerald, and re sells the ring for a profit on ebay. In this case there is also some value added for know-how on ring values and jewelry repair.

Seen another way, arbitrage is the process of taking to the market a difference in price between two products, at a profit, hopefully.

Another simple example of arbitrage would is if Stu buys a lot of 10 printers at close out in Best Buy for $1,000, and then proceeds to sell them individually for $150 on the Craig's List website. Hence, if he sells all of them, he creates a $500 arbitrage profit.

Arbitrage can encompass going through more than one step in obtaining a profit from a product.

For example Carly is a businesswoman who has access to buy 100 gallons of gasoline in Country A for two dollars per gallon. She has also found out that ball pythons can be legally imported and sold in Miami for $100 each. So with $200 she buys 100 gallons of gasoline in Country A, transports it to Country B, and exchanges it, with her animal dealer contact, for 25 ball pythons. She then transports the snakes to Miami and sells each for $100, for a total of $2,300, because two died on the way. She invested $200, plus transport cost, plus her time, and received more than 10 times back.

Sounds great… well, yes.. However, there are a couple of risks you have to be aware of. Just to mention some of the problems that could have arisen:

- The gasoline could have been contaminated and been worthless

- The contact in Country B may not have needed gasoline

- The contact in Country B ran out of snakes

- More snakes could have died on the trip

- Snakes could have become illegal in Miami

- A large shipment of pythons arrived two days before in Miami, and they are now worth $1 each.

Hence, arbitrage can be very profitable, but can also be a failure if not carefully analyzed, planned, and executed. Assurance of the final demand is fundamental.

Arbitrage is commonly used in financial transaction. For example: Brian sees the following exchange rates at one time:

$1.45 per Euro

$1.60 per English Pound

.40 British Pound per Euro

So he quickly buys 625 English Pounds with $1,000. Then he buys 1,562 Euros with his English Pounds. He then buys $1,077 with his 1,562 Euros. He ends up generating $77 profit on currency arbitrage. These types of transactions are done, by large institutions and countries, automatically with computers that monitor currency fluctuations, on a daily basis, and for millions of $.

Another case of arbitrage can be created when betting odds are different at two locations. For example: There is an important tennis match between tennis team Green and tennis team Blue. Stacy wants to make some money by betting on the match. She notices that at location A, the match has 1 :1 odds. In other words, if you bet on a team and that team wins you double your money. At Location B she sees that they believe team blue has a lot less chance to win. They are paying 2:1 odds on team Blue. In other words, if she bets on team blue at location B she triples he money. So Stacy does her arbitrage calculation, and decides to make some easy money. She bets $300 dollars on team Green at location A, and $200 on team Blue at location B.

If team green wins she wins $300 at location A, but losses $200 at location B, in other words, she nets $100. If team Blue wins she wins $400 at location B, but losses $300 at location A, also netting $100. Either way she plays, she wins $100, using arbitrage.

Arbitrage is everywhere around us, and pops up as opportunities in time. It can be very profitable if risks are analyzed and evaluated. Be on the constant lookout for these opportunities. Usually they are short lived, but with good training, you can make a lot of money using arbitrage.

"Everything should be made as simple as possible, but not simpler."

Albert Einstein

Chapter 6

Compartmentalize

This technique has proven very effective in dealing with a multitude of problems at a given time. The more the method is used the more effective it becomes. When dealing with a number of problems at the same time, we tend to become multi-taskers, where we try to solve all the issues at the same time. This usually leads to poorly thought out planning and mediocre results. In fact, by doing this, we can be attempting to correct situations that have not been properly identified.

Compartmentalizing is opposite of multitasking. The point is to isolate each problem and focus energy and resources on just one issue at a time.

This process can be described as breaking up the larger problem into individual smaller problems, and placing each smaller problem in a cabinet. Mentally put that problem into a compartment and close the door on it. To work on the individual project, open the door to that cabinet and dedicate all your energy and focus to working on that issue.

For example: You have project A, project B, and project C, due on the same date, and the amount of work required to complete them is overwhelming.

Solution: Create three mental, or even physical, compartments. Each compartment will be labeled (project A, project B, and project C). Open one cabinet and focus on working on that project.

At any point you can close the door on this compartment and move on to the next. Once a door is closed on a compartment we must try to put it out of our mind. The better we can do this, the more we can dedicate our concentration and vigor to the next compartment. Close all the doors and take some time for rest and internal peace; it will help with clarity of mind when you open each compartment again.

As you break down the problems and work on each individual one with possible solutions, several things will happen: you will see the problem and possible outcomes more clearly; solutions will be easier to find; and by breaking up the problem and solving small parts of it, positive progress to an overall solution will be made!

While this technique seems exceedingly simple, it is difficult to master. However, it is invaluable in organizing and sorting through all kinds of situations in our daily lives.

"If someone feels that they had never made a mistake in their life, then it means they had never tried a new thing in their life..."

Albert Einstein

Chapter 7

The Pitfall of Self – Destruction

Man, or any thinking creature for that matter, seeks to find his level of comfort. Once this level is achieved, the mentality changes to maintenance of his status-quo.

A simple example of this would be when a person arrives home from work and finds his house temperature is a warm 80 degrees, so he turns the thermostat down to a comfortable 72 degrees. Once his house has cooled, he changes his focus to maintaining this level of satisfaction. Once his home is cool he sits on the sofa and accepts any other small temperature miss-comforts because it is "good enough" and the effort to get up and change it further is more trouble than its' worth.

Why is this a problem?

In more important issues in life, and in business, this "good enough" can be a major problem...

Let me illustrate with another example, where bigger risks are involved...

A mountain climber is ascending a mountain. His goal is to reach the peak. As he climbs, he has a few slips, but these are dealt with as part of his ascent; He regains his footing, and his focus remains steady. His sharp senses and skills keep him on track for his mission. Each step has a purpose, and is carefully planned.

Once he reaches the peak he rests, and admires his climb. He thinks about the luck he had, because all the conditions were right for him to achieve his goal. As he relaxes, a storm blows in. He slips, and starts sliding down the mountain. He tries a few things to brake his fall, but he continues to slide. When he understands that these counter measures are not being effective to stop the slide, he starts to panic and tries riskier strategies. But these riskier strategies are untried and un-proven, and end up accelerating his fall. He is now in a growing snowball that does not stop till it reaches the bottom of the mountain.

In a similar way, if a businessman or woman, sets as his goal to reach sales of $1 million, he will probably achieve it. When goals are well set and thought out, they are very achievable, and usually accomplished. He uses steady steps, focus, confidence, and determination in traveling this path.

In this chapter, my focus is more on what may happen once the goal is achieved, rather than the process of achieving it...

My experience has been that once the goals are reached, the mindset changes. The drive to push further with strength, wanes, and complacency and restful satisfaction increase. I think this is part of human nature. Determination of purpose is gradually replaced with thoughts of protection of achievements. This is actually a very dangerous place to be, because there will be storms that come, and they can catch you sitting. Suddenly, you can be the snowball at the bottom of the mountain with little comprehension of what happened.

The initial slippage is subtle and difficult to perceive. Once a goal is achieved, the mentality changes to how lucky we were that the conditions were right, and that the achievement was due more to external conditions, rather than our persistence and determination. Self doubt creeps up as a silent killer. We gradually lose confidence and our sharp skills dull. A storm can now push us with more ease into a slide than when were climbing.

As the slide accelerates, self doubt and desperation sets in and our counter measures are panic driven and lack conviction and sharpness. Very easily we can turn into a snowball that grows and ends up at the bottom. My experience has been that the climb takes years, but the slide happens in months or even days. As human nature would have it, as we get higher, the voice grows stronger that tells us that there is a big drop below us. And as we reach the top, that voice is telling us that there is only one way to go from here... down.

So how do we stop this sleeping dragon of self destruction from awakening? I believe that the direction can be derived from habits of "super-achieving" individuals. Their mindset difference is simple, but against human nature. As soon as their goal is reached, they set a new higher goal, with little time for complacency and admiration. They embark on this goal immediately to keep their skills sharp and maintain focus. They strive to keep their hunger and drive as the prevalent voice.

It is for this reason, I think, that they don't stop at $1 million, or $10 million, or even a billion. They continue to push themselves to higher levels as soon as the last level was achieved.

If we use this experience to teach us, we must retrain our mindset to keep continually driving toward greater goals, fighting constantly against the looming voice of how high we are, and how much we can fall. Our focus and pleasure must be in the constant climb, not on reaching the goal.

In summary, I recommend to all of you, to always set a new peak as soon as you reach your current one. As in the case of the alpinist, as soon as he climbs one mountain, he must think of the next, and continue to train and sharpen his skills.

Begin climbing to this goal immediately, and be very cautious about stopping to look back and admire your achievements, lest you lose focus and drive.

However, if you should slip along the way, and the storm comes around, be particularly thoughtful and sharp. Greater skills are required to stop the slide and re-initiate the ascent than those that were used to reach the summit the first time, because of the self-doubt and panic that accompany this situation. And even on the occasion that you find yourself in a snowball at the bottom of the hill, remember that you have the skill to climb, and that you have learned something from your last trek. Re-train, re-focus, drive yourself anew, and start climbing.

Chapter 8

Cash Flow

Cash flow is defined as the movement of cash into and out of your pocket, or bank account. Money flows into your pocket when you earn it, and flows out when you spend it. In order to pay for things we have to have enough money coming in to cover their cost. Think of it as a bathtub, with two hoses; one hose where the water comes in (cash in) and another where the water flows out (cash out). If more water comes into the bathtub than goes out, the bathtub will fill; if more water goes out than is coming in the bathtub water level will go down, possibly, till it is empty.

Any business transaction will have a certain amount of money going out and a certain amount of money coming in. Business success is defined as more water coming in than is going out, and business failure is defined as more money going out than is coming in.

Before and during any business activity it is important to evaluate, and plan that more money will come in than is going out. This is referred to as positive cash flow. Negative cash flow, on the other hand, is when there is more money going out than coming in.

Investment

An investment is when you bring in money from another source in order to create or improve a positive cash flow. For example, in the case of purchasing a business, the money paid to buy the business is the investment. For a business to be a success, the cash flow from the business must be enough to cover the cash flow going out, including money to return the initial investment.

Example:

You have a possibility of buying a business for $100,000 that has total cash sales of $200,000 and total cash expenses, including taxes of $150,000 (cash out). You have to borrow the $100,000 to buy the business from a friend, who in return for making the loan, expects a yearly payment of 10% interest, and $10,000 toward the loan amount (in 10 years you would have paid your friend the total $100,000). Is this a good deal?

First, you must determine the net cash flow for the business. This is done by subtracting the cash out from the cash in. In this case, total cash in: $200,000 minus total cash out: $150,000, equals positive net cash flow per year of $50,000.

Next, you must figure out how much you have to pay your friend for the loan; 10% interest on $100,000 equals $10,000 per year, and you must also repay $10,000 of the loan amount each year. Hence your friend will receive $20,000 for the first year.

So, from your net cash flow of $50,000, you pay your friend $20,000 and you have $30,000 of cash left over. This is good a good business deal.

Compound Interest

Interest is defined as money you make when you lend, and money you pay when you borrow. The percentage rate you make, or pay, is called the interest rate.

If you borrow money, you will pay interest based on an interest rate, plus you will repay a portion of the principal amount (loan amount).

A deposit you make in a savings account in a bank, will earn you an interest rate on that money. The interest rate will vary depending on several factors, among them; how safe is the borrower, how safe is the place where the money will be held, and the overall state of the economy. If you deposit money into savings account that pays 10% per year, each year you will receive 10% of interest on your money.

In the case that you leave the money in a savings account for several years, you have the benefit of receiving compound interest.

Example:

You deposit $1,000 into a savings account that pays 10%. Here is how your money would grow each year.

Year	Interest Rate	Interest $ received	Account Balance
1	10%	$ 100	$ 1,100
2	10%	$ 110	$ 1,210
3	10%	$ 121	$ 1,331
4	10%	$ 133	$ 1,464
5	10%	$ 146	$ 1,611
6	10%	$ 161	$ 1,772
7	10%	$ 177	$ 1,949
8	10%	$ 195	$ 2,144
9	10%	$ 214	$ 2,358
10	10%	$ 236	$ 2,594

At the end of ten years, you would have $2,594. Your money would have doubled somewhere between the seventh and eighth year. The huge benefit is that you are receiving new interest on top of the interest you earned in the previous year. This is compound interest, also known as compound growth.

The Rule of 72

The rule of 72 is a simple way to calculate the amount of time that would be required to double your money, in the case of a compound interest payment. The number 72 is divided by the interest rate you are paid, and the result is the amount of time necessary to double your money.

If you use the example above, and divide the number 72 by the 10% interest per year, the result will be 7.2 years. Your money will double in 7.2 years.

The Rule of 78

If you borrow money in order to buy a car or a house, the bank will probably calculate your payments based on the rule of 78. This formula makes the interest portion of the debt a large percentage of the initial payments. The formula is derived by adding the numbers from 1 to 12 (78), assuming monthly payments for one year as the denominator, and then applying the inverted month number as a numerator.

In other words, the interest portion of the first month is $12/78^{th}$ of the total interest; the interest portion of the second month is $11/78^{th}$, and so on, till the twelfth month, where the interest portion would be $1/78^{th}$.

On home loans, or car loans, after a few years, the principal balance has changed very little; since you have been paying most of the interest on the loan in the early years.

If you pay the loan in the period specified, the total interest will turn out to be the same as if you had paid the same amount each year, however should you sell or pay off the loan early, the bank gets the enormous bonus of having collected a large portion of the total interest on the loan. It is difficult, but if possible, avoid this type of loan.

In summary, cash flow is the lifeblood of business. We must strive to have more water coming into the bathtub, than is going out, to be successful.

"The most powerful force in the universe is compound interest"

Albert Einstein

Conclusion

You have now been exposed to many interesting concepts that are part of everyday knowledge in the business world.

Take additional time to study and learn more about business concepts as you move forward in life. All aspects of our daily lives are touched in some form by business, hence the more you know, the more protected, balanced, and prepared you are.

Albert Einstein saw the power of compound interest not only as it applied to money, but as it applies to life. If you spend a little more time in study each day, the cumulative effect is enormous as knowledge is built upon knowledge. I have seen case after case, from athletes, musicians, and businessmen that are enormously successful because of a cumulative effect of a small additional dedication each day.

Take the time to build on yourself, on your knowledge and your abilities, to improve yourself and the world around you.

"Try not to become a man of success, but rather become a man of value."

Albert Einstein

www.ingramcontent.com/pod-product-compliance
Lightning Source LLC
Chambersburg PA
CBHW021023180526
45163CB00005B/2081